25 Emergent Reader Plays Around the Year

BY CAROL PUGLIANO-MARTIN

SCHOLASTIC
PROFESSIONAL BOOKS

NEW YORK • TORONTO • LONDON • AUCKLAND • SYDNEY
MEXICO CITY • NEW DELHI • HONG KONG

To Dorothy and the students in Dorothy and Carol's
First-Grade Class at Little Red School House
for endless inspiration and motivation.

Cover design by Norma Ortiz
Cover and interior artwork by Tammie Lyon
Interior design by Kathy Massaro

ISBN: 0-439-10564-1

 # Contents

Introduction

Oral reading is an important part of any reading program. Providing children with frequent opportunities to read aloud to their classmates helps them gain confidence and feel comfortable speaking in front of others. It is also a way for teachers to observe students' reading ability and progress without having to read one on one with each child. (This can be particularly difficult when one teacher is responsible for as many as 30 students!)

However, there has been recent debate about a widely used oral reading activity, known as "round-robin reading," in which students sitting in a circle take turns reading aloud to the rest of the group. Round-robin reading can often inhibit, rather than encourage, children's oral reading. They may compare themselves to others in their group, often with negative consequences. Students may also become more self-conscious because they may feel that the focus is on their reading skills rather than on the content of the text.

The plays in this book provide early readers with an alternative to round-robin reading. Children are more motivated to read aloud when they feel they are contributing in a meaningful way, rather than just because they are next in the circle. Each child can think, "This is my part. Therefore, it is my turn to read." They realize that their part adds to the play's plot and they feel a sense of purpose. Children are often less inhibited when they are reading parts in a play because they are working together. The focus is on the efforts of the group rather than on the reading ability of individuals.

My first-grade reading group has greatly enjoyed reading plays. Although the plays are designed for oral reading rather than for performance, they work well for either purpose. For variety, I have tape-recorded the children reading aloud and then played the tape back as they follow along in the text. They become very excited at hearing their own voices on tape. I have also played the tape while children make puppets of characters for a later performance. The taped reading provides inspiration while students work on the puppets and also reinforces the words in the play.

I hope that this book provides you with a valuable learning and assessment tool. I also hope that these plays will allow your students to celebrate their newfound reading talents and to read for the sheer enjoyment of letting their voices be heard.

Carol Pugliano-Martin

CURRICULUM CONNECTIONS

Fall

Back at School!

Challenge your class to create new lines about being back at school. Follow the pattern of the play by starting each line with a letter of the alphabet (A is for…, B is for…, and so on). Since the play ends with the letter H, you may wish to have students begin with the letter I. Can they make it all the way to Z? Once the children are finished with their lines, invite them to make torso-sized letter cards that they can wear around their necks while they perform the play for themselves or for another class. You may also want to perform the play at a back-to-school assembly or another special event. This group activity will help build a sense of community early in the year. Afterward, display the alphabet cards for year-round reference.

Fall Is Coming

After reading the play, discuss the different signs of fall. Ask: "In the fall, what changes do we see in nature? What special things do people do in the fall?" (pick apples, drink cider, look at leaves, and so on) Write the following categories on chart paper: Seeing, Hearing, Touch, Smell, Taste. Ask children to brainstorm the various ways we use each of our senses to enjoy the fall. Write their ideas under each heading. Then divide the class into five small groups and assign each group a different sense. Invite each group to write a poem or story about using one of the senses during the fall. Encourage students to use the ideas written on the chart.

A Day in the Pumpkin Patch

This play touches on an important theme: that living creatures grow in different ways. To explore this theme with a fun activity, gather a bunch of small pumpkins or gourds of different sizes, shapes, colors, and textures. Divide the class into small groups and have them spread out from one another. Give each group a pumpkin, making sure that others can't see what it looks like. Have each group carefully observe the pumpkin and write down a detailed description of it. They can even weigh the pumpkin and measure its height and circumference. When students are finished, collect the descriptions and line up the pumpkins where everyone can see them. Label the pumpkins with numbers or letters. Invite volunteers to read the descriptions aloud. Ask students to listen carefully to each description and then write which pumpkin they think is being described. Finally, have groups reveal the answers.

Spider's Surprise

Invite your class to create a mock newscast of the new way Spider acts in this play. To prepare for this activity, ask students to watch a news program at home, or have them watch an afternoon broadcast as a class. Students can play different roles, such as news anchor(s), reporter(s), Spider, and the insects who were freed from Spider's web. The news anchor(s) can start the activity by introducing the story. The reporter(s) can then interview the various characters. Have other students ask the characters questions as if they are in a news conference.

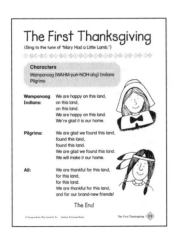

The First Thanksgiving

Find four or five pictures of scenes from the first Thanksgiving. Try to find pictures that show different aspects of the event, such as Native Americans, Pilgrims, meal preparation, feasting, game-playing, and so on. *The First Thanksgiving* by Jean Craighead George (Philomel, 1993) is an excellent source for illustrations. Divide your class into groups, and give each group a picture. Have each group take turns freezing in the pose depicted in the picture. On the count of three, encourage group members to bring their picture to life. They can add dialogue to their scene or simply do movements. If only one person is in a picture, each child in the group can play the same part simultaneously.

Old Friends, New Friends

The beginning of school is not only a time for seeing old friends but also a time to meet new ones. A good way to break the ice is to have students conduct a classroom survey. In advance, prepare survey sheets with a list of questions such as "Like pizza? Have a dog? Play soccer?" Provide a long line beside each question. Distribute survey sheets to students and ask them to go around the room "surveying" their classmates. When a child answers yes to a question, he or she then writes his or her name or initials on the line beside the question.

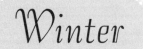

Time to Hibernate

Have a class discussion about hibernation. Ask children to think of animals that hibernate, and list their responses on chart paper or on the chalkboard. They will probably guess several mammals. Then find a book about hibernation and read it to the class. *What Do Animals Do in Winter?: How Animals Survive the Cold* by Melvin and Gilda Berger (Chelsea House Publishers, 1998) is a good choice. Children will discover that mammals, such as chipmunks, are not the only animals that hibernate; reptiles, amphibians, and even some insects hibernate as well. Invite each student to research a hibernating animal, including the animal's habitat, diet, and so on. Have students then make shoe box dioramas to show what they have learned. For example, a chipmunk's diorama would include dried leaves, grass, and acorns. A lizard's habitat would include rocks. Display the dioramas in your school or local library to encourage others to read about animals that hibernate.

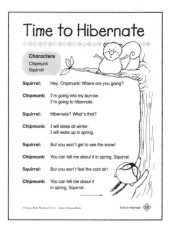

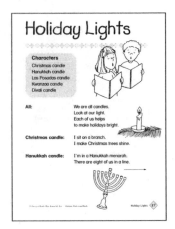

Holiday Lights

Lights are an important part of winter celebrations. Ask students to name other important aspects of their holidays, such as family, food, decorations, activities, and so on. Ask children to bring in magazines from home. Invite students to look through the magazines for images that remind them of their holiday celebrations. (Magazines from November and December will have a lot.) Have students cut out all the images and then work together to make a classroom mural by gluing the pictures onto a large sheet of craft paper. Then challenge children to think of categories for the different images (such as family, food, and lights). List the categories on chart paper. Have students count the images that fall under each category and write the results on the chart paper. Which category had the most images? Which one had the least? What did they learn about the holiday celebrations?

Roll, Roll, Roll the Snow!

Explain to students that snow consists of tiny crystals. Here is a fun experiment to make your own crystals and observe how they form. You will need:

- black crayons
- dark construction paper
- hot plate
- saucepan
- $1\frac{1}{2}$ cups water
- goggles
- 2 cups Epsom salts
- teaspoon
- wooden spoon
- small paper cups
- paintbrushes or cotton swabs
- magnifying lenses

Distribute crayons and construction paper to students. Ask them to draw a simple picture, and then put their drawings aside. Add $1\frac{1}{2}$ cups water to the saucepan. Place the pan on the hot plate and bring the water to boil. Have students put on goggles and take turns adding 1 teaspoon of Epsom salts to the water. Encourage students to observe the change in the Epsom salts as they are added. After each student has had a turn, add any remaining Epsom salts. Stir carefully until the salts dissolve. Remove the pan from the hot plate and allow it to cool. Pour a small amount of the solution into paper cups. Invite students to dip a paintbrush or cotton swab into the solution and brush it over their drawings. Have students use magnifying glasses to carefully observe the crystals forming as the solution dries.

Watch That Groundhog!

Invite students to write and illustrate a newspaper article about Groundhog Day. First bring in a few newspapers so that they can look at the format. Discuss the purpose of headlines and have them come up with a headline for their article. Provide some suggestions such as "Groundhog Sees Shadow!" or "Early Spring Ahead!" As a group, brainstorm ideas for their articles. Explain that news articles tell what happened, where and when it happened, and who was involved. Challenge children to answer these questions in their articles and to be creative in coming up with details. They can then write and illustrate their articles, working individually, in pairs, or in small groups. When children are finished, you may wish to compile the articles into a class newspaper. Invite children to come up with a name for their paper. You can even choose a computer font that resembles one used in the local newspaper.

100 Days of School!

Hold a 100th day of school count-a-thon! Divide your class into small groups of about four or five. Ask each group to decide upon an item that they can collect 100 of, such as small stones, bottle caps, pennies, beads, or macaroni. Then have students determine how many items each group member will contribute so that they are divided up equally (or as close as possible). Once children have brought in the items, ask group members to take turns counting the objects. For example, the first student counts from 1 to 20, the next student counts from 21 to 40, and so on. After they have counted by ones, have students count by twos, fives, and tens. When they are finished counting, invite groups to make a 100th Day display by gluing their objects onto a piece of posterboard. Encourage them to arrange the objects into groups of five or ten. Hang the displays in the hallway to get the whole school in the 100th day spirit!

Valentine Love Bugs

Use this play as a springboard to study insects. Ask students if they know what makes an insect. (Insects' bodies have three parts: head, thorax, and abdomen. They also have six legs, and many species have wings.) Have students name as many insects as they can and list their responses on the board. How do they know they are insects? Find some books that have photographs of many different insects so that students can determine whether the animals on their list are insects. Encourage them to compare various insects in the books. How are they alike? How are they different? You may want to discuss with your class that many small creatures like spiders and ticks are not insects. They belong to a different class of animals called arachnids.

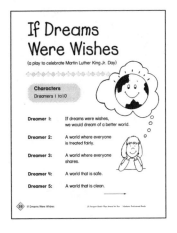

If Dreams Were Wishes

This play is based on first graders' actual wishes for a better world. To inspire your students to think of their own wishes, read aloud Dr. Martin Luther King Jr.'s "I Have a Dream" speech. (You may also wish to show your students a video of the speech.) Explain that Dr. King uses the word *dream* to describe his wishes for a better world. Ask children to think of wishes that would make our world a better place. Then explain to them that sometimes people carry signs to let others know their wishes. Invite students to write their wishes on signs. They can work individually, in pairs, or in small groups. Organize a march around the school in honor of Martin Luther King Jr.'s birthday. Explain to students that Martin Luther King Jr. encouraged peaceful ways, such as marches, to spread the word about civil rights.

Signs of Spring

After reading the play, have a discussion about the various signs of spring. Can children think of any other signs of spring, besides the ones in play? Have each child make a "Signs of Spring" journal in which they can record the changes that take place during the transition from winter to spring. Give students each two or three pieces of white paper and ask them to fold the paper in half. Then show them how to stack the pages so they look like a book. You may wish to help students bind their books by stapling along the fold.

Invite children to write a title on the cover and decorate it with drawings. Have them bring their journals outside on various occasions to record the changes they observe. Ask them to draw what they see, write about it, and label it with the date. When they finish their books, children will be able to look back at the progression from cold, wet weather to bright, sunny springtime!

Spring Cleaning Time!

How about Spring Cleaning Time in your classroom? Having kids help clean and organize their classroom helps to foster respect for the room and its belongings. Together, brainstorm a list of spring cleaning tasks and write them on chart paper. These might include washing shelves, cleaning pet cages, organizing supplies, cleaning out cubbies, sharpening pencils, and even changing wall displays. Have students collaborate to write new verses for the play based on the list. Divide the class into groups and invite each group to choose a cleaning task. Before the cleaning begins, read the new verses together to build enthusiasm. When all the tasks are finished, celebrate with a spring cleaning party!

Springtime on the Farm

Invite students to draw a picture of an animal that lives on a farm. Children can use the animals in the play or perhaps come up with an animal that is not mentioned. Have them read about the animal and write a few interesting facts about it. Then divide the class into small groups. Play charades by having each group take turns acting out the animal of their choice while others guess. If possible, arrange a trip to a local farm so that the class can see the farm animals up close. It may be the first time some of the children have seen these animals. Children can then see for themselves if their charade depictions were close to how the animals actually behave.

Why Can't Every Day Be Earth Day?

As a class, brainstorm a list of things that children can do to help the earth every day, such as recycling, conserving water and energy, not littering, and so on. Invite your class to imagine that they are the kids who are cleaning up the pond in the play. What would they tell the animals when they ask them, "Why can't every day be Earth Day?" Collaboratively write another ending to the play to tell how they would answer this question. Encourage children to use the ideas that they brainstormed. How will the play end? Will the animals be satisfied with their ideas? Or will children have to think of other solutions?

Frog Watch

Use this play to introduce a study of animal life cycles. Using the frogs as an example, discuss the concept of life cycles. As a class, brainstorm a list of animals that includes reptiles, birds, and mammals. Divide the class into small groups and have each group choose an animal from the list and research its life cycle. Provide students with books and magazines about animals.

Invite students to make life cycle wheels to show what they learned. Model for children how to make the wheels by following these directions. Use a pencil to poke a hole through the center of two paper plates. Draw lines to divide one plate into four equal sections. Illustrate one stage of the animal's life in each section. The sections can show the animal growing, eating, being nurtured by its parents, and so on. Place the second plate on top of the first so they nest together. Cut out a window in the top plate so that one complete section will show through. Use a brass fastener to connect the wheels, placing the one with pictures behind the other. As children turn the top wheel, they can review each stage of their animal's life cycle.

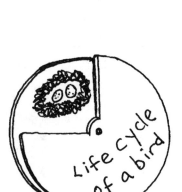

The Stars and Stripes Speak Out

Before reading the play, ask your class if they know what the stars and stripes on the American flag stand for. Write their ideas on chart paper, and then read the play. After reading, use an almanac or encyclopedia to examine flags from other nations. If there are children in your class from other countries, or if students have family members or friends from other countries, it would be interesting to look at their nations' flags. Open a discussion about what the different symbols on those flags might represent, and write children's ideas on chart paper. Then divide the class into groups and invite each group to research one flag. Challenge students to find out the actual meaning of their flag's symbols. Ask groups to share their findings, and add the information to the chart. What message does each flag communicate through its symbols? How are the flags alike and different?

Summertime Is Almost Here!

The games in the play are only a few activities that can be enjoyed during the summer. After reading the play, ask children what else they like to do when they are out of school. Show students how they can use these ideas to make up their own verses. As each child contributes an idea, add that verse to the song. Then sing all the verses together!

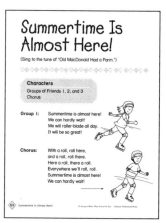

Hello and Good-bye!

Divide the class into two teams, the "hello" team and the "good-bye" team. Ask the "hello" team to make up their own verses of things they are looking forward to during the summer. The "good-bye" team makes up verses about what they will miss about school. Teams can work together, in small groups, or individually. When they are finished, have the teams sit together and take turns sharing their verses. Later, they can illustrate their verses and compile them into a class book entitled "Hello and Good-bye!"

Light Up the Night

For this play, you may wish to provide the firefly character with a flashlight. The firefly can then flash the light while reading the lines "Blink! Blink!," "Twinkle! Twinkle!" and "Flash! Flash!" At the end of the play, allow small groups of students to take turns performing a "Dance of the Fireflies"! Ask children if they have ever observed fireflies twinkling at night. Do all of the fireflies flash their lights at the same time? Are the flashes staggered? Does the light stay on for long or is it a quick flash? Give each child in the group a flashlight. Make your room as dark as possible, and put on music that evokes fireflies, such as classical or New Age. Encourage children to move around the room, flashing their lights as they move. Note how the children play off of each other. Do they take turns flashing the light? Do some children flash repeatedly and others infrequently? Rotate groups until everyone has had a turn. Enjoy your ready-made summer night!

The Seashell

Whether your students have ever been to a beach or not, they will surely be fascinated by a collection of shells kept in the classroom. Try displaying them at the beginning of the year, to ease children from summer to back-to-school time. Keep your shell collection in your science area near magnifying lenses, so that children can wander over and view the different shells up close. For a more formal activity, invite children to view the shells under a magnifying lens, draw what they see, and write what it looks like to them. You can also use shells for sorting and classifying. How many different ways can children sort and classify the shells? Draw several Venn diagrams on large sheets of construction paper. Write categories on the diagram about the shells' size, shape, color, and texture. Then ask children to place shells in the appropriate places on the diagram.

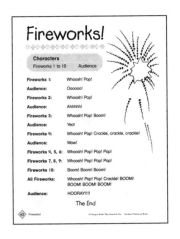

Fireworks!

This play uses only the sounds of fireworks to portray this exciting event. After reading the play a few times, invite students to perform the play using sounds made from found objects. They can look around the classroom and experiment with making different sounds, or they can look for items at home to recreate the sounds in the play. For example, students can pop balloons, squeeze empty plastic milk jugs, crumple brown paper bags, shake sheets of oaktag, and so on. After they have performed the fireworks play using their sound objects, encourage students to come up with other ideas for a "sound play." Some examples might include a storm (dry rice in a shoe box makes a good rain sound), the seashore, an amusement park, and so on. Many of the objects used in the fireworks play may be adapted for the new play; other sounds may require new objects.

I Swim, You Swim!

Invite your students to imagine that they are scuba diving deep in the sea. Ask them what they think they might see. What kinds of creatures might they find? What might the plants look like? Provide students with books that show pictures of underwater life. Make a list of sea creatures that students find in the books. Then spread a large sheet of craft paper on the floor and pass out pencils, crayons, and watercolors. Encourage students to draw and paint an underwater scene. They can include themselves, sea creatures, plants, submarines, coral reefs, and even a lost underwater world!

Back at School!

Characters

Letter A	Letter D	Letter G
Letter B	Letter E	Letter H
Letter C	Letter F	

Letter A: A is for…an apple for teacher.

Letter B: B is for…because we're back.

Letter C: C is for…can you believe it?

Letter D: D is for…did you bring your backpack?

Letter E: E is for…everyone is ready.

Letter F: F is for…finding friends is cool.

Letter G: G is for…great to see you!

Letter H: H is for…happy to be back at school!

The End

Fall Is Coming

Narrator 1:   Fall is coming.
Look at the trees.

Trees: Our leaves are slowly changing color.
They will turn red, orange, and gold.

Narrator 2:   Fall is coming.
Feel the wind.

Wind: I am getting cooler every day.

Narrator 1:   Fall is coming.
                  Look up in the sky.

Birds: We are flying to a warmer place.

Narrator 2:   Fall is coming.
                  Look at the sun.

Sun: I wake up later in the morning.
                  I go to bed earlier at night.

Narrator 1:   Fall is coming.
                  Look at the children.

Children: We are getting ready to go back to school.

All: Fall is coming!

The End

A Day in the Pumpkin Patch

Characters

Pumpkin	Sprout 1
Scarecrow	Sprout 2
Crow	Sprout 3

Pumpkin: I'm a lonely little pumpkin.
Boo-hoo! Boo-hoo! Boo-hoo!

Scarecrow: Why are you boo-hooing?

Crow: We really want to know.

Pumpkin: Because I'm the only pumpkin here.
I'm the only one to grow.

Scarecrow: Don't worry, you won't be lonely
for long. ⋯⋯⋯➤

Crow: Soon, other pumpkin sprouts
                 will come along.

Sprout 1:   Stretch! Hello!

Sprout 2:   Pop! Good morning!

Sprout 3:   Boing! How do you do?

Scarecrow: Hey! Look who's here!

Crow: Just like we told you.

Pumpkin: I'm so glad that you are here.
                 I couldn't wait anymore.
                 What was all of that waiting for?

Sprout 1:   Some pumpkins grow quickly.
                 Others take longer.

Sprout 2:   Some pumpkins are weaker.
                 Others are stronger.

Sprout 3:   Each pumpkin grows in its own way.
                 And each way of growing is okay.

Scarecrow: You will all keep changing
a bit every day.

Crow: You will all be ripe pumpkins
by Halloween day.

All: We will be the brightest pumpkin patch
that people have ever seen.
And we will wish them all
HAPPY HALLOWEEN!

The End

25 Emergent Reader Plays Around the Year Scholastic Professional Books

Spider's Surprise

Characters

Narrator 1	Spider	Grasshopper
Narrator 2	Bugs	Beetle
	Bee	Ant

Narrator 1:   The itsy, bitsy spider
was getting set for Halloween.

Spider: I'll surprise the other bugs this year!

Narrator 2:   The bugs asked . . .

Bugs: What do you mean?

Narrator 1:   Spider turned to look at them.
He scratched his spider head.

Spider: I won't play spider tricks on you.
I'll give you treats instead!

Narrator 1: A bee flew into Spider's web.

Bee: I think my days are done!

Narrator 2: But Spider let the bee go free and said...

Spider: Hey, this is fun!

Narrator 1: Along came Grasshopper and Beetle.
Then came tiny little Ant.

Narrator 2: They all went into Spider's web.
Spider began to chant...

Spider: I'll set you all free today.
Enjoy it while it lasts.
I'll be back to my old ways
When Halloween has passed.

The End

25 Emergent Reader Plays Around the Year   Scholastic Professional Books

The First Thanksgiving

(Sing to the tune of "Mary Had a Little Lamb.")

Wampanoag Indians:
We are happy on this land,
on this land,
on this land.
We are happy on this land.
We're glad it is our home.

Pilgrims:
We are glad we found this land,
found this land,
found this land.
We are glad we found this land.
We will make it our home.

All:
We are thankful for this land,
for this land,
for this land.
We are thankful for this land,
and for our brand-new friends!

The End

Old Friends, New Friends

Characters

Friends 1 to 8

Friend 1: Do you like your old friends?

Friend 2: Shy friends, bold friends,
how we love our old friends!

Friend 3: Sweet friends, neat friends,
walking down the street friends.

Friend 4: Good friends, glad friends,
help you when you're sad friends.

Friend 5: How about some new friends?

Friend 6: New friends, true friends,
lots of things to do friends.

Friend 7: Hey friends! Hello friends!
It's great to know you friends.

Friend 8: Near friends, far friends,
we're so glad we have friends!

The End

Time to Hibernate

Characters

Chipmunk
Squirrel

Squirrel: Hey, Chipmunk! Where are you going?

Chipmunk: I'm going into my burrow.
I'm going to hibernate.

Squirrel: Hibernate? What's that?

Chipmunk: I will sleep all winter.
I will wake up in spring.

Squirrel: But you won't get to see the snow!

Chipmunk: You can tell me about it in spring, Squirrel.

Squirrel: But you won't feel the cold air!

Chipmunk: You can tell me about it
in spring, Squirrel.

Squirrel: But you won't slide around on the ice!

Chipmunk: You can tell me about it in spring, Squirrel.

Squirrel: Chipmunk?

Chipmunk: Yes, Squirrel?

Squirrel: What is it like to hibernate?

Chipmunk: I'll tell you about it in spring, Squirrel.

The End

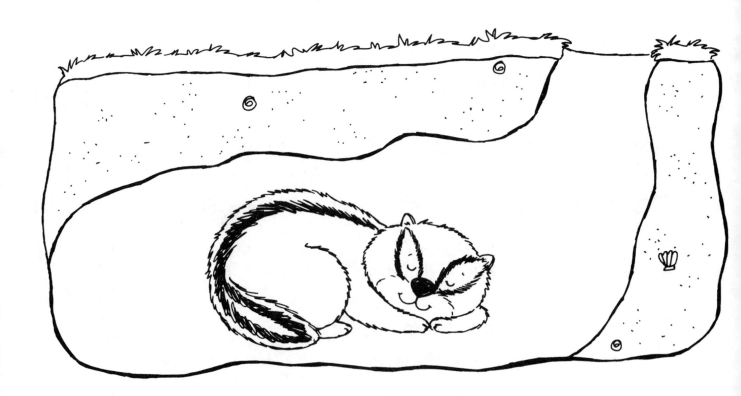

25 Emergent Reader Plays Around the Year   Scholastic Professional Books

Holiday Lights

Characters

Christmas candle
Hanukkah candle
Las Posadas candle
Kwanzaa candle
Divali candle

All:

We are all candles.
Look at our light.
Each of us helps
to make holidays bright.

Christmas candle:

I sit on a branch.
I make Christmas trees shine.

Hanukkah candle:

I'm in a Hanukkah menorah.
There are eight of us in a line.

Las Posadas candle: I celebrate Las Posadas.
Children carry me at night.

Kwanzaa candle: I'm in a Kwanzaa kinara.
Just look at my light!

Divali candle: On Divali, I sit
in a lamp made of clay.
Then I'm placed in a window
to help light the way.

All: We are all used
on different holidays.
But even so,
each of us makes
our own holiday glow.

The End

25 Emergent Reader Plays Around the Year   Scholastic Professional Books

Roll, Roll, Roll the Snow!

(Sing to the tune of "Row, Row, Row Your Boat.")

Characters

Snowball Roller 1

Snowball Roller 2

Snowball Roller 3

Snowball Roller 4

Snowball Roller 5

Snowball Roller 1: Roll, roll, roll the snow.
Make a big snowball.
Make two more and stack them up
so that they won't fall.

Snowball Roller 2: Roll, roll, roll the snow.
Each arm will be a stick.
One on the left, one on the right,
that will do the trick!

Snowball Roller 3:   Roll, roll, roll the snow.
Add some button eyes.
Now he's looking right at me.
What a nice surprise!

Snowball Roller 4:   Roll, roll, roll the snow,
a carrot for the nose.
Make a mouth out of some coal.
Now we need some clothes!

Snowball Roller 5:   Roll, roll, roll the snow.
Add a scarf and hat.
We have made a great snowman,
And that's the end of that!

The End

Watch That Groundhog!

Characters

Groundhog	Raccoon
Squirrel	Skunk
Bear	

Groundhog: I am a Groundhog and I'm here to say, please watch me on Groundhog Day.

Squirrel: Why should we watch you? What do you do?

Groundhog: I'll let you know when winter will be through.

Bear: How can you do that? Please let us know.

Groundhog: I come up from the ground to look
for my shadow.

Raccoon: What if you see it?
What happens then?

Groundhog: We'll have six more weeks of winter,
my friend.

Skunk: And if you don't see it,
what will that bring?

Groundhog: That means we'll have an early spring!

Squirrel: Wow, Groundhog. We can't wait!

Bear: Will spring come early?
Will it be late?

Raccoon: Get back in your hole.
Then get ready to come out.

Skunk: We'll be waiting without any doubt.

Groundhog: Good-bye for now. I'm on my way.
I'll see you all on Groundhog Day!

The End

100 Days of School!

Characters

Students (or Groups) 1 to 9

Student 1:   100 days of songs to sing.

Student 2:   100 days of bells that ring.

Student 3:   100 days of everything!

Students 1, 2, 3:   100 days of school!

Student 4:   100 days of stories told.

Student 5:   100 days of pets to hold.

Student 6:   100 days is pretty old!

Students 4, 5, 6:   100 days of school!

Student 7:   100 days of reading fun.

Student 8:   100 days of jobs well done.

Student 9:   100 days for everyone!

Students 7, 8, 9:   100 days of school!

The End

Valentine Love Bugs

Characters

Ant	Cricket
Bee	Love Bug Group 1
Fly	Love Bug Group 2

Ant: Sorry, I'm late.

Bee: That's okay.
I just got here, too.

Fly: Let's begin our
Bug Club meeting.

Cricket: Wait! Look! Who are you?

Love Bug Group 1: We are the Love Bugs.

Ant: Love Bugs?

Bee: What are Love Bugs?

Love Bug Group 2:   We are cute little bugs.

Love Bug Group 1:   We look like hearts.

Love Bug Group 2:   We came to say hello
                                       before our job starts.

Fly: What is your job?

Love Bug Group 1:   Love Bugs come out once a year.
                                       We help spread Valentine's Day
                                       cheer.

Cricket: Do you bite?

Love Bug Group 2:   No, we kiss.

Ant:	Do you sting?
Love Bug Group 1:	No, we hug. That is how we spread love.
Bee:	Sounds good to me. Would you like to join our Bug Club?
Love Bug Group 2:	Sure! But now we must be on our way.
Love Bug Group 1:	It's time to spread love on this Valentine's Day.
Fly:	Good-bye, Love Bugs!
Cricket:	Hey, you know what? I love you guys!
Ant:	Hey! Those Love Bugs really do their job!

The End

If Dreams Were Wishes

(a play to celebrate Martin Luther King Jr. Day)

Characters

Dreamers 1 to 10

Dreamer 1: If dreams were wishes,
we would dream of a better world.

Dreamer 2: A world where everyone
is treated fairly.

Dreamer 3: A world where everyone
shares.

Dreamer 4: A world that is safe.

Dreamer 5: A world that is clean.

Dreamer 6: A world where people respect one another.

Dreamer 7: A world where people live in peace.

Dreamer 8: A world where people are kind to animals.

Dreamer 9: A world without hate.

Dreamer 10: If dreams were wishes, we would keep dreaming ...

All Dreamers: ... until all our dreams came true!

The End

Signs of Spring

Characters

Robin	Tulip	Sun
Bud	Grass	

Robin: I am a robin.
I am the first sign of spring.

Bud: I am a bud on a tree.
I am the first sign of spring.

Tulip: You are both wrong.
I am a tulip.
I am the first sign of spring.

Grass: No, no, no!
I am a blade of grass
I am the first sign of spring.

25 Emergent Reader Plays Around the Year   Scholastic Professional Books

Robin: Let's ask the Sun.
The Sun will know which one of us
is the first sign of spring.

Bud: Sun, can you help us?
I say that I am the first sign of spring.

Tulip: And I say that I am.

Grass: No, no, no! I am!

Robin: I am!

Sun: Why are you fighting?
It doesn't matter who is first.
You are all important!
Now, let's make this the best spring ever!

All: Ready, set, spring!

The End

Spring Cleaning Time!

Characters

Spring Cleaners
1 to 9

Spring Cleaner 1:   Clean all the windows.
Make sure that they shine.

Spring Cleaner 2:   Wash all the curtains.
Hang them on a line.

Spring Cleaner 3:   Dust off the shelves.
Don't they look just fine?

Spring Cleaners 1, 2, and 3:   It's Spring Cleaning Time!

· · · · · · · · · · · · ➤

Spring Cleaner 4: Mop all the floors.
Shake out all the rugs.

Spring Cleaner 5: Clean the kitchen cabinets.
Wash the plates and mugs.

Spring Cleaner 6: Throw away old food,
so there won't be bugs.

Spring Cleaners 4, 5, and 6: It's Spring Cleaning Time!

Spring Cleaner 7: Clean out all the closets.
Give away old clothes.

Spring Cleaner 8: Polish all your shoes,
so that each one glows.

Spring Cleaner 9: Throw out all your junk,
'til the trash can
overflows.

All: It's Spring Cleaning Time!

The End

Springtime on the Farm

Characters

Farmer	Lamb	Calf
Hen	Cat	Duck
Chicks	Cow	Ducklings
Sheep	Kittens	Piglets

Farmer: I am so excited!
Spring is really great.
So much is going to happen.
I can hardly wait!

Hen: After sitting on my eggs,
I just hatched some chicks.

Chicks: Now we're snug and cozy
in our nest of straw and sticks.

Sheep: Come and meet my little lamb.
He's almost fast asleep.

Lamb: When I grow up I want to be
the biggest woolly sheep.

Cat: I just had some kittens.

Cow: And I just had a calf.

Kittens and Calf: And when we play together,
everyone has a laugh!

Duck: Look at all my ducklings.

Ducklings: All we do is quack.

Piglets: We piglets cannot wait until
our next yummy snack!

Farmer: It's great to be a farmer,
especially in spring.
Meeting lots of brand-new friends
is such a special thing!

The End

Why Can't Every Day Be Earth Day?

Characters

Skunk	Beaver 2	Duck
Beaver 1	Baby Beaver	Frog

Skunk: Hey, Beavers! Where are you going?

Beaver 1:   We're moving to another pond.

Beaver 2:   It's too dirty here.

Baby Beaver: Yuck!

Skunk: What do you mean?

Beaver 1:   There is too much trash in the water.

Beaver 2:   We keep bumping into cans and boxes.

Baby Beaver: Ouch!

Duck: I know what you mean, Beavers.
But today is Earth Day.

Frog: Turn around. The kids from the school
are cleaning up our pond.

Beaver 1:   So they are!

Beaver 2:   It looks better already!

Baby Beaver: Yea!   ·················➤

Beaver 1:	But…
Skunk:	But what?
Beaver 1:	What about when Earth Day is over?
Beaver 2:	Yes. What will happen then?
Baby Beaver:	Uh-oh.
Duck:	Let's go talk to the kids.
Frog:	What will we say?
Duck:	We'll ask them, "Why can't every day be Earth Day?"
All:	Let's go!

The End

Frog Watch

Characters

Tadpole/Frog 1   Tadpole/Frog 3   Tadpole/Frog 5
Tadpole/Frog 2   Tadpole/Frog 4

Tadpole 1:   Pssst!
                  Hey, tadpoles!

Tadpole 2:   Yes?

Tadpole 3:   What is it?

Tadpole 1:   We are being watched.

Tadpole 4:   Look at all the kids!

Tadpole 5:   Why are they watching us?

Tadpole 1:   They want to see us turn into frogs.

Tadpole 2:   How long have they been watching?

Tadpole 1:   Since we were eggs, I guess.

Tadpole 3:   Well, let's give them a good show!

Tadpole 4: Boys and girls! Step right up to Frog Watch!

Tadpole 5: Watch us tadpoles turn into frogs!

Tadpole 1: Some of us are starting
to grow legs.

Tadpole 2: In a few weeks, we will all have legs
and no tails!

All Tadpoles: We will be frogs!

A few weeks later…

Frog 3: Welcome back to Frog Watch!

Frog 4: As you can see, now we are all frogs!

Frog 5: We hope you enjoyed our show!

All Frogs: Ta-da!

The End

The Stars and Stripes Speak Out

Characters

Flag   Child   Stars   Stripes

Flag: Hello, there!

Child: Who, me?

Flag: Yes, you.

Child: Who is talking to me?

Flag: I'm up here, on the wall.

Child: The flag?

Flag: Yes, I'm glad you finally noticed me.

Child: What do you mean?

Flag: Well, every day you come to school.
Here I am on the wall.
But you never notice me.

Child: You're right. I'm sorry.

Flag: Do you know about me?
Do you know why I have stripes?

Child: Umm ... no.

Flag: Stripes, please tell about yourself.

Stripes: Before there were states in this country,
there were 13 colonies.
Each of us stands for a colony.

Child: Oh, I see.

Flag: How about the stars?
What do you know about them?

Child: Hmm … well …

Flag: Never mind.
Stars, please tell about yourself.

Stars: There are 50 stars on the American flag.
Each of us stands for a state.

Child: Oh, I see! Hey, flag?

Flag: Yes?

Child: You're pretty cool.

Flag: Thank you for noticing!

The End

Summertime Is Almost Here!

(Sing to the tune of "Old MacDonald Had a Farm.")

Characters

Groups of Friends 1, 2, and 3
Chorus

Group 1:   Summertime is almost here!
We can hardly wait!
We will roller-blade all day.
It will be so great!

Chorus: With a roll, roll here,
and a roll, roll there.
Here a roll, there a roll.
Everywhere we'll roll, roll.
Summertime is almost here!
We can hardly wait!

Group 2:   Summertime is almost here!
We can hardly wait!
We will play hopscotch all day.
Let's all celebrate!

Chorus: With a hop, hop here,
and a hop, hop there.
Here a hop, there a hop.
Everywhere we'll hop, hop.
Summertime is almost here!
We can hardly wait!

Group 3:   Summertime is almost here!
We can hardly wait!
We will play leap frog all day.
Hurry, don't be late!

Chorus: With a leap, leap here,
and a leap, leap there.
Here a leap, there a leap.
Everywhere we'll leap, leap.
Summertime is almost here!
We can hardly wait!

The End

Hello and Good-bye!

Characters

Students 1 to 10

Student 1:   Hello to the warm days of summer.

Student 2:   Good-bye to the great days at school.

Student 3:   Hello to playing in sunshine,
and jumping in pools to get cool.

Student 4:   Good-bye to a favorite teacher,
and friends we would see every day.

Student 5:   Hello to days that are longer,
which will give us more time to play.

Student 6:   Good-bye to working together,
and sharing things that were fun.

Student 7:   Hello to helping at home more.

Student 8:   Good-bye to classroom jobs well done.

Student 9:   Though we are saying good-bye now
to school and to our friends,

Student 10:   soon we will be back here,
saying hello once again!

The End

Light Up the Night

Characters

Narrator 1	Bee	Ladybug	Firefly
Narrator 2	Ant	Grasshopper	

Narrator 1: One day the insects were talking.

Narrator 2: They were bragging about what they could do.

Bee: I can buzz very loudly!
BUZZZZZZ!

Ant: Oh yeah? Well, I am very strong.
I can carry heavy leaves.

Ladybug: That's nothing. I help farmers.
I eat bugs that can hurt their crops.

Grasshopper: I can play music.
I rub my wings together to make songs.

Bee: Hey, Firefly! What can you do?

Ant: Firefly? He can't do anything.

Ladybug: Yeah. Just look at him. He's
nothing special.

Narrator 1: Firefly said nothing.
He thought for a moment.

Firefly: I can light up the night.

Grasshopper: What? No, you can't!

Firefly: Meet me in the field after dark.
I will show you.

 25 Emergent Reader Plays Around the Year Scholastic Professional Books

Narrator 2:	So the insects met in the field after dark.
Bee:	Where is Firefly?
Ant:	Maybe he tricked us into coming.
Firefly:	Blink! Blink!
Ladybug:	Hey look at that!
Firefly:	Twinkle! Twinkle!
Grasshopper:	It's Firefly!
Firefly:	Flash! Flash!
Bee:	How beautiful!
Ant:	Firefly, we are sorry.
Ladybug:	You were right.
Bee, Ant, Ladybug and Grasshopper:	You really do light up the night!

The End

The Seashell

Characters

Beachcombers 1 to 9
Seagull

Beachcomber 1: I found a tiny seashell
sitting in the sand.

Beachcomber 2: I picked it up and brushed it off.
I held it in my hand.

Beachcomber 3: What creature lived inside of you?
What creature called you home?

Beachcomber 4: What creature carried you around
when it was time to roam?

Beachcomber 5:   A seagull looks inside you when
it wants something to eat.

Seagull: I hope that inside this shell
I'll find a tasty treat!

Beachcomber 6:   Sorry, Mr. Seagull.
You're not in luck today.

Beachcomber 7:   Whatever lived inside this shell
has left and gone away.

Beachcomber 8:   I will not keep you, little shell.
I'll put you back and then,

Beachcomber 9:   whatever lived inside of you
might come back home again!

The End

Fireworks!

Characters

Fireworks 1 to 10   Audience

Fireworks 1:   Whoosh! Pop!

Audience: Oooooo!

Fireworks 2:   Whoosh! Pop!

Audience: Ahhhhh!

Fireworks 3:   Whoosh! Pop! Boom!

Audience: Yea!

Fireworks 4:   Whoosh! Pop! Crackle, crackle, crackle!

Audience: Wow!

Fireworks 4, 5, 6:   Whoosh! Pop! Pop! Pop!

Fireworks 7, 8, 9:   Whoosh! Pop! Pop! Pop!

Fireworks 10:   Boom! Boom! Boom!

All Fireworks: Whoosh! Pop! Pop! Crackle! BOOM!
                          BOOM! BOOM! BOOM!

Audience: HOORAY!!!!

The End

I Swim, You Swim!

Characters

Swimmers 1 to 15

Swimmer 1:   I swim.

Swimmer 2:   You swim.

Swimmer 3:   We all swim.

Swimmer 4:   We love to swim!

Swimmer 5:   I swim at the beach.

Swimmer 6:   I swim in a pool.

Swimmer 7:   We all love to swim.

Swimmer 8:   When we swim we stay cool!

Swimmer 9:   I swim like a frog.

Swimmer 10:   I swim like a fish.

Swimmer 11:   We would choose to swim

Swimmer 12:   if we had only one wish.

Swimmer 13:   I swim.

Swimmer 14:   You swim.

Swimmer 15:   We all swim.

All: We love to swim!

The End